— Dorothy's —
Simply Beautiful
Flowers

CRANE HILL
PUBLISHERS

Copyright © 2003 by Dorothy McDaniel
Book design by Miles Parsons
All illustrations by Tim Rocks, except pages 48–50 by Ernie Eldredge
Flower arrangements photographed by Keith Harrelson
Flower identification photographs by Michael McDaniel

Published by Crane Hill Publishers
Printed in Italy

Library of Congress Cataloging-in-Publication Data

McDaniel, Dorothy, 1941-
 Dorothy's simply beautiful flowers : a step-by-step guide to simple
sophisticated arrangements / Dorothy McDaniel.
     p. cm.
Includes bibliographical references.
 ISBN 1-57587-212-9 (alk. paper)
1. Flower arrangement. I. Title.
 SB449.M28 2003
 745.92--dc22

                              2003016556

For more information about flowers and arrangements online visit
www.dorothymcdaniel.com

10   9   8   7   6   5   4   3   2   1

Dorothy's
Simply Beautiful
Flowers

Dorothy McDaniel

CRANE HILL
PUBLISHERS

Acknowledgments

Thanks to the following for their help with this book:

Marcia Unger Interior Design
Jane Hoke—Hawkins Israel
Sandra Najjar
Lance Spangler—Salon Raymond Barry
Leza Duncan
Chris Carter—Christopher Glen
Sara Scholl Interior Design
Maude Morgan
Joyce Lichtenstein

I want especially to acknowledge my son, Michael McDaniel, who has been with me since my first shop in 1977. He has always shared my love of flowers and encouraged me to share my ideas.

Also, I would like to extend thanks to my staff for their support and contributions:

Tana Avery
Chris Burson
Anne Cardwell
Daniel Grayson
Gena Hyatt
Clevell Johnson
Vona Keeling-McDaniel
Carter Kennedy
Melissa Lepore
Tiffany Nowell
Kay Ramey
Bud Watson
Julie White
Paul Zwack
Buddy Robbins
Alan Townsend

Table of Contents

A Life Full of Flowers

I never imagined that I would own a flower shop, since I studied sociology and criminology in college. But in 1975, while teaching part-time at the University of Alabama at Birmingham and raising three boys, Michael, Peyton, and Pete, my marriage ended and life changed.

I had long been doing flower arrangements for friends for special occasions, using flowers from my own garden and local wholesale houses. As time went on, the demand for my services grew, and it became obvious that I would either have to go into business or out of friends. So, in November 1977, I opened a small flower boutique in a house on Linden Avenue in Homewood, a suburb of Birmingham. The building included several businesses, and my space was about twelve feet by fifteen feet. I bought an old work table, a few display items, and a second-hand Pepsi-Cola® cooler from the local bottling company. A friend painted a few flowers on a sign, we placed it over the "Ya-hooo! Mountain Dew" logo on the cooler, filled it with as many tulips, daisies, roses, irises, and amaryllis as would fit, and that was the beginning. The cooler came with a lifetime service guarantee and a pledge to move the cooler whenever necessary. True to their word, the bottler moved the cooler five times and serviced it until I finally sold it a few years ago.

Twenty-six years later, I'm still in the flower business, and I love it. My shop, "Dorothy McDaniel's Flower Market," is located just a few blocks from that first boutique, but at 6,000 square feet, it's quite a bit larger. I'm thankful every day to be in a business where I am surrounded by such beauty. I'm still amazed when the flowers come in by air from places such as Colombia or Holland, and they're both stunning and affordable.

Looking back, I realize that flowers have always been an important part of my life. I grew up in a large Greek family. My father, Peter Michael Sarris, immigrated to Birmingham from his native Tsitalia, a small village in southern Greece, when he was 14 years old. He met my mother, Nicoletta (better known as Lena), through relatives, and they were married in 1941. I have two younger sisters, Dena and Tena (yes, they are twins), and lots of aunts, uncles, and cousins.

My parents had a garden with shrubs and fruit trees, including pomegranate, pear, peach, plum, and fig. We had plenty of annuals and perennials for cutting. Mother says I often gathered the flowers from her garden and brought them in to her. She loves flowers, as did my grandmother, and I attribute my passion to their influence. I remember Mother grew marguerite daisies, pansies, roses, and sweet peas. I loved the little sweet peas. Mother grew them on lattice, and I just remember they were soft and lovely, and not everybody had them. Mother always had a few fresh flowers on the table and, for special occasions, we bought arrangements from the neighborhood florist.

I recall with joy so many childhood events shared with family and friends; all were festive because four ingredients were always present: great food, live music, Greek dancing (which everyone joined in because there was no need for a partner), and beautiful flowers.

I remember when I was a young bride living in Atlanta, there was a convenience store near our home that was owned by a woman who brought lovely flowers from her garden to sell nearly every day. After doing my marketing, I would stop at her place and pick up bunches of Queen Anne's lace, daisies, or bachelor's buttons to take home. They always made me happy, and they still do.

For me, flowers are a constant in a world that is rampant with change, an assurance of sorts that there is order to the universe. Every spring, crocuses pop up from a thawed winter ground. No matter what, dogwoods herald Easter, roses permeate my home with sweetness in summer, and the chrysanthemums light up the fall with blazes of color.

I have spoken to hundreds of groups about floral arranging over the years, and friends and others have often encouraged me to write down my ideas. So I decided (finally) to do this book. I've witnessed dramatic changes in the industry in the quarter century since I opened my first shop. Flower cultivation has become international, with varieties coming from every corner of the world and, increasingly, from countries with abundant labor. The net result is that every imaginable kind of flower is available in many locations—supermarkets, street stalls, and, of course, flower shops—and the prices are affordable.

Also in the past 25 years, people's tastes in home decorating have become more sophisticated (due in part to increased travel and television), and more people are interested in surrounding themselves with fresh flowers of all sorts. The trick for many is having the time and the know-how to do the arranging (thus, the popularity of the "grab-and-go" pre-wrapped bouquets). At the same time, entertaining has become much more relaxed. That's why I have focused this book on arrangements that are simple yet beautiful, unfussy yet sophisticated.

There are countless books available with extraordinary flower arrangements. I know, because I own most of them. The problem is that they offer little practical advice for those who want to learn basic flower arranging skills. My intention is for this book to be just that – a primer of the basics. Since I have always adhered to the adage that "a picture is worth a thousand words," I have included a DVD that contains visual instructions to supplement the book's text.

I hope that my approach to arranging will inspire you to bring more fresh flowers into your home. When you do, you'll realize how much joy flowers can add to your life.

Here's to Beautiful Flowers,
Ειζ τα ομορφα λουλουδια!
Dorothy McDaniel

Getting Started

Sometimes, the hardest part of any project is knowing where to begin. Flower arranging is no different. The key to success is knowing the basic steps and following them.

Before beginning any arrangement, you'll need to do a few things: First, determine the place for the arrangement. Next, select a container. Now you're ready to select the flowers you will use. You'll also need to make sure you have the tools and supplies you need. On the next few pages, I cover each of these steps in detail, including a list of tools and what they're used for, along with some basic facts about flowers and arrangements.

— Steps for Success —

Select the spot

Be innovative. Consider unusual places for your arrangements—places that are unexpected. Don't ever do an arrangement and then try to find a place for it. It is the space that dictates the size, the color, and the shape. Ideally, the arrangement should be created where it will be placed. By doing that, you can see the necessary proportion and needed shape, and make adjustments as you go. This is particularly important for beginning arrangers.

For example, an arrangement that will sit on a table against the wall should be basically three-sided, since the back will be unseen; an arrangement for a round seating table should have circular flowers that can be viewed from all sides. It is important not to obscure the views of the guests who will be seated at the table (tall flowers can work if they are above eye level and are dramatic). If the surface where the arrangement is to be placed could be damaged by moisture, be sure to put some kind of cloth over the area while you are arranging.

Choose a container

Choosing a container for flowers is a lot like selecting the right frame for a beautiful painting. The color of the container must complement the space, and size and shape must be considered as well. The occasion will also help determine container choice. If it is a formal occasion, then silver, pewter, porcelain, or cut glass may be good choices. If the event is casual, then pottery, earthy baskets, bright plastic, or just ordinary clay pots would be appropriate.

For any arrangement, a clear glass container is always a good choice. Glass never competes with the flowers, and clear glass is available in nearly every conceivable size and shape.

Test your container to be sure it holds water. If it does not, but you really want to use it, try to find a glass or even a plastic cup or vase that will fit down inside to hold the water or the floral foam. Another way to line porous containers is to use round or oval

plastic liners. They are inexpensive, widely available wherever floral supplies are sold, and come in every size — from four inches to eighteen inches in diameter. If the shape of the container does not lend itself to liners, a heavy plastic bag will work because you can mold it to the shape of the container.

I always enjoy using clay pots for arrangements. They can be used for both casual and formal settings. They are readily available in garden shops, grocery stores, and flower shops, and they come in hundreds of sizes, from one inch in diameter to sixty inches in

diameter. There are also liners available in most of those sizes. I particularly like the rose pots because they are taller and a little sleeker, but still available in a lot of the same sizes. I'll often place a clay saucer under the pot and, depending on the setting, I will fill the space between the pot and the liner with sheet moss.

Some flower vessels are obvious, but almost anything that has an opening can be adapted to hold flowers. We have a wire bustier in our shop that we have lined with a glass vase and filled with flowers to be used at lingerie showers, in powder rooms, and for various other occasions. For baby showers and births, we often fill small wagons, carriages, baby cups, or even toy cars with flowers. Recently for a bridal luncheon, we placed several vintage purses (all of which could stand alone) on the table, lined them, and filled the liner with floral foam and then with flowers. We paid only a few dollars for the containers at a nearly new shop and achieved a unique look.

The more you work with flowers, the more likely you will find vases that work well in the spaces you like to have flowers. Invest in a few containers that afford you easy arranging possibilities, and that you can always rely on. Then be very creative in your choices when you have the time to experiment. Finally, be sure that your container is the right size for the flowers you have available. A common mistake is choosing a container that is too big for the number of stems. Most arrangements work better in containers with smaller openings if you are not using floral foam, because you have more control.

Another idea is to use several containers that are all the same size or several different sizes and shapes to form an arrangement. Here are a few examples: Use three identical cylindrical vases in three different heights and cluster them to form one centerpiece; use five silver julep cups to march down a table; or use seven or nine bottles of various sizes and colors, each holding one stem.

Choose your flowers and greenery

There really are no rules for choosing flowers. Like art, you should buy what you love and don't worry a lot about matching your decor. There are, however, certain flowers that can have a more casual effect (gerberas), or a more formal appearance (roses). There are also certain colors that are more complementary in certain rooms. For example, an all-white arrangement is stunning in a room with deep red walls. But an arrangement of reds, oranges, and hot pinks — a monochromatic range of color — can be fabulous if the arrangement is not against the wall, but on a table in the room.

Bear Grass

Color is important in any display, so think it through and experiment with different color combinations in your home. Be daring!

The commercial flower market is so international today that more and more flowers are available year 'round. They are also fresher because of how quickly they can be shipped directly from the grower. The result is that you get a fresher product almost any time you want it, for a reasonable price. The chart on pages 76-77 of this book lists many commercial

Pittosporum

flowers and their availability. If you do not find what you are looking for, ask your local florist to order it. Even in small towns, with ample notice, this shouldn't be a problem.

Aspidistra

In larger cities, expect to find a good selection in supermarkets, flower stalls, and large flower shops. If you want specific flowers or colors for a special arrangement, it is best to order them and have them available when you need them. There are some flowers that are truly seasonal, and I do not recommend using them out of season. Even though they might be available, they are likely to be poor quality and more expensive. An example is tulips, which are available from October until the end of May. After that, shipping is a problem because of the heat. Tulips do not fare well in heat, and the blooms are likely to be small and of inferior quality. Remember, if you are planning an event and you have your heart set on a certain flower, check availability. Otherwise, for best quality, choose flowers that are in season.

Salal

As for greenery, there are a number of desirable greeneries available on the commercial market. I prefer green or variegated pittosporum, miniature pittosporum, salal, aspidistra leaves, and bear grass. There are ,however, many available greeneries in most yards. Explore your yard and cut a few greens and condition them by soaking in water to determine if they last well, then experiment using them in your arrangements.

— Tools of the Trade —

Before you get started, you need to have a few basic tools and supplies. These are essential to easy arranging. Most of these items can be found at flower shops and stores that carry art and craft supplies. These retailers typically also sell floral supplies, as do some hardware stores.

Floral scissors. Keep these on hand exclusively for cutting stems and thin wires. Under $20.

Knife. Useful for cutting stems and floral foam. You can use any straight-edged knife to cut foam, but to cut stems, you'll need a small, sharp knife devoted only to that purpose. This can have a fixed blade or a folding one. The latter is better because it can be tucked in lots of places for outdoor flower-gathering expeditions. Quality will determine price. Get a good one that can be sharpened and will last a long time.

Pruning shears. Use to cut and shape heavy stems from trees to use in arrangements. Be sure to keep all your cutting tools sharp because dull tools can crush stems. Quality will determine price.

Simply beautiful secrets ————

Floral foam explained

Often referred to by the popular brand name Oasis®, this hard green sponge-like material is used to hold flower stems inside a container. You'll be amazed at the versatility it gives you.

Instant foam has little holes in it and is fast saturating, while deluxe foam takes longer to saturate. Instant is satisfactory for most table-size arrangements, but if heavy stems or branches are added, the arrangement may require deluxe. Large arrangements with lots of flowers also need to be reinforced with chicken wire. Never push the foam down into the water; let it submerge naturally.

Green floral tape. Strong and waterproof. It must be put on a dry surface, but once it is secured, water will not affect it. It is generally used to secure floral foam to a container. About $8.95 a roll.

Clear floral tape. Useful for making grids over the openings of vases and bowls. Flowers are then inserted in the openings made by the grid. This is particularly helpful if the container has a large opening, because it gives you better control. $3.99 – $5.99.

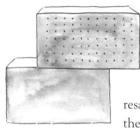

Floral foam. There are two types, lightweight (instant) and heavy duty (deluxe). It is sold in blocks and is a green, spongy substance that absorbs water and is used to secure stems in a container. Never reuse foam; it won't resaturate properly, and it will introduce bacteria in the old foam to your fresh flowers. Costs about $2 for a 3x4x9" brick.

Simply beautiful secrets ─────

Use clear tape for quick flower control
To help position your flower stems in a vase or other container, try making a grid across the mouth of the vase using clear floral tape. Simply crisscross pieces of tape from one side of the opening to the other, leaving holes the size of your stems, or just slightly smaller, in between. Insert the stems in the holes and your arrangement will magically stay in place! Use sprigs of greenery if you need to hide any tape ends.

Floral picks. Green pointed wooden sticks for wiring fruit into bunches. Also used to add stability to stems when sticking into foam. About $.03 – $.05 each.

Foam rings. Great to have for a festive door wreath of fresh

flowers, or to place on a table with a candle in the center. Prices vary with size; expect to pay $8 minimum, and up to $50 for the really large ones.

Floral wire. There are many lengths and gauges of wire, but for most home uses, 21-gauge is all that you will need. This can be used to wire heads of flowers that need support. About $0.15 per wire.

Roll wire. Roll wire is great to have on hand for making garlands and securing them to railings, or securing arrangements to mailboxes or other items. About $12.99.

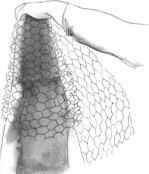

Chicken wire. Hexagonal wire mesh. It is two feet wide, and usually sold by the foot. Floral supply retailers will also have green coated wire made especially for flowers. Strong and flexible, chicken wire can be placed over floral foam to support heavy branches and stems, or used for inserting many stems into a small space. It can also be balled up and stuffed into a container to help support stems. Be sure to tuck in loose ends. Also, do not use in any container made of silver or other materials that could be scratched by the wire. About $2 a foot, and it can be reused.

Green pipe cleaners. These are great for securing bouquets before dropping them into a container when foam is not used. You can also use them to secure the heads of flowers when making topiaries. They come in boxes of 100 that cost about $8. Reuseable.

Raffia, ribbon, and string. These are useful for binding materials together or adding decorative touches to topiaries or other arrangements.

Frogs. Ceramic or metal forms that secure flower stems in a vase. They are available in a variety of shapes and sizes at equally varying prices. Some are a cluster of dense needles or metal points that can be placed inside a container, with flower stems then secured on the points. Others are metal grids to stick the stems between. I even have one in my shop that is a green frog with holes in the center. For whimsy, I'll use it inside a glass container, put flowers in the holes, and the frog becomes part of the arrangement. I also have some antique frogs that are so interesting that I place them in shallow containers and use only a few flowers in them so that the frogs show.

Simply beautiful secrets

Tool tips

Be sure that clippers, or any floral cutting tools, are used only for that purpose and are kept clean and sharp. Otherwise, they will damage the stems. Woodsy stems may require pruning shears to make a clean cut.

Glue gun and florist glue. A glue gun is a great tool for securing fabric to an inexpensive plastic container or empty jelly jar, or attaching ribbon to the perimeter of a market basket to cover the rough edges. Glue guns are now available with cool glue, which I recommend for home use. I have lost a few layers of skin when hot glue has dripped from one of the hot guns. The cool glue is perfect for securing leaves to the exterior of a container for a great natural look.

Storage container for floral supplies. I use a large plastic toolbox to hold most of my supplies. They are portable and have trays and sections for sorting things. I keep my floral foam in a clear plastic box with a top to protect it.

— Simple Arrangement Ideas —

Think about flowers for arranging in three categories: line flowers, face flowers, and filler flowers. Line flowers are tall, spiky flowers like larkspur, snapdragons, or bells of Ireland; face flowers are flowers that have a big fat face, like gerberas, peonies, lilies, or roses; and filler flowers are small, leafy flowers like Queen Anne's lace, waxflower, solidago, or hypericum.

The hardest arrangements to master are those that mix all three types of flowers. But you can make it simple. Beginning with the placement of some greenery around the perimeter, add line flowers first, then face flowers (you can use more than one variety), and then filler. If any floral foam shows, add a little more greenery. Don't over-green because it detracts from the flowers. Draw an imaginary triangle with each type of flower you have placed (for instance, your placement of gerberas should form a triangle within the arrangement). If your triangles all are complete, then the distribution is correct.

❀ Cluster three containers of different heights and put flowers of the same color in each container. Each vase should contain a different size flower. A good rule of thumb is to have about two inches difference in the height of the containers, and the same difference in the finished height of the flowers.

❀ A vase of two dozen cool-blue delphiniums can make a wonderful large display. Easy!

❀ Use one flower in different colors, like a vase full of snapdragons in light pink, medium pink, magenta, and apple, which is a pink and white bi-color snap.

❀ Line up seven bottles on a table, all clear or all one color, such as blue. Put different blue flowers in each bottle. Put the tallest flower in the center, then let the size get smaller as you go out to each side.

❀ Here's a quick creative idea. Take six empty soda bottles, add water, and place them in their carton. Put one gerbera daisy in each bottle. This arrangement relies on a monochromatic color scheme for impact, so make the flowers the same color as the carton. If their faces are drooping, you may have to wire them. (Insert wire into head of flower, and wrap around the stem as you go down.) Then stabilize them by inserting a sprig or two of greenery into the bottles next to each stem.

Simply beautiful secrets

How to select the best bouquet in a grocery store
When selecting flowers in the grocery store, check their proximity to produce. Certain types of produce emit ethylene gas, which is detrimental to flowers. Also, flowers that are held outside a cooler do not last as long as those stored in a cooler. Check flowers that are in a wrapper by carefully sliding the wrapper down to expose the heads. If they have been in a wrapper long, they could have moisture trapped inside, which causes mold and deterioration. Always check for yellowing foliage and translucent petals, which indicate age or damage.

— Make It Last —

When you buy flowers, look them over carefully to be sure they are in good condition. Yellowing foliage is a sign of age or damage. Slimy stems or foliage indicate old age or poor care. Flower heads like lilies that are creased or translucent are damaged or old. If you are not in a rush, buy flowers such as lilies as they are just beginning to show color. They will last longer, and it is a pleasure to watch them open. Although florists and markets usually display their flowers in water, preferably in a cool environment for maximum life, they will dry out in the time it takes to get home. So put them in water right away.

It is essential that you give all the flowers a fresh, slanted cut, underwater if possible, and place them immediately in water with floral preservative (available from all florists) until you want to arrange them. The slanted cut allows the maximum surface for absorbing water. Be sure your buckets and containers are very clean. Fill them with tap water into which floral preservative has been dissolved.

Always use the preservative, not only when conditioning the flowers, but also in the finished product. It helps increase the life of the flowers, and also keeps the water clean. For maximum enjoyment, cut the stems every couple of days and change the water. It was once thought that crushing woodsy stems such as forsythia or magnolia assisted in their water intake. But now we know that it creates trauma that may damage the stem. It is best to give these stems a sharp, angular cut and treat them like other flowers.

Easy Tabletop Arrangements

Here are the five basic steps to absolutely perfect arrangements for any tabletop, along with some ideas for adorning the table once you've placed the flowers. Then I'll show you how to make my three favorite tabletop arrangements.

☀ Step I

What is the occasion? Before putting together a dining room table arrangement for a special event in your home, you'll need to answer a couple of questions. Will people be seated at the table or will they be standing around it? Is it a casual or formal occasion? If people are seated, you want them to be able to see over or around the flowers. If people are standing, as at a buffet, you'll want to use an arrangement with more height and substance.

Step 2

Select the container or containers (review hints for this in *Getting Started*, page 11).

Step 3

Choose the flowers and greenery.

The appointments in the room should help determine which flowers you select. For instance, if your dining room has busy floral wallpaper, select one flower from the wallpaper, one color, and do a mass of that one flower. That will complement the wallpaper and also be very striking. If your walls are painted, consider a monochromatic arrangement that sharply contrasts with the wall color, or coordinates with it.

Step 4

Decide if you'll need just water, or if the container needs floral foam (see "Tools of the Trade," in *Getting Started*, page 17).

Step 5

Arrange the flowers in the container.

Some arrangements are exceptions to this, but as a general rule, put in the greenery first, then add an anchor for the flowers, then add the flowers.

Simply beautiful secrets ─────────

Blending flower colors

I tend to believe that most colors work well together, depending on the setting. I do have some personal favorites: red, orange, and hot pink for a great monochromatic range; purple, red, and yellow for a vibrant display; peach, light blue, and cream for a soft color palette; or for a refreshing look, all white and green.

The last step for a tabletop design is to determine what — if anything — should be on the table with the arrangement. Here are a few of my favorite ideas.

Flowers are a great addition for a luncheon place setting. I like using napkin rings that are designed to hold a small flower. Select a flower from the arrangement, or one that is complementary. I also like to make tiny arrangements and put one at each place, so each person has their own flowers. You can use a 1" pot with a bit of floral foam inside it, then add flowers and even a place card.

Simply beautiful secrets

Longer life for flowers

To get the most out of your arrangements, recut stems when you get home, underwater if possible, and use flower preservative (available wherever floral supplies are sold) in the water. Repeat this every two or three days, cleaning the vase and using fresh water each time. The brief time it takes to accomplish this will produce dramatic results.

Candles are a lovely addition in the evening. If your table is long, you can use three staggered candlesticks on either side of the flowers. Just be sure that they are higher or lower than the arrangement, not the same height.

You can surround the arrangement with sherbet glasses and put floating candles in them, or you can add votive candles to the table. Traditionally, candles are to be lit only after five o'clock. I believe there are exceptions to that rule. In the South in July, it is daylight until eight o'clock, and it's hot and humid. I think candles are a poor choice. In December or January, using candles on a cold, dreary winter morning makes perfectly good sense. I say use your good judgment, and your imagination.

Do you have a collection of figurines you want to show off? Nestle them around your arrangement. Do you have some beautiful shells? Arrange them artfully around a centerpiece of all  blue flowers to give the idea of cool water. I have a collection of porcelain teacups. No two are alike, but they all look good together. I often arrange them on a large tray on my sideboard, putting flowers in three of them and using the others for coffee or tea service.

Now you are ready to go on to three of my favorite tabletop arrangements that are simple, but sure to wow your guests.

Roses in Cups

For a seated dinner, this works wonderfully.

You'll need: five short opaque containers (I use silver julep cups),
30 roses, greenery for each cup, pipe cleaners, and floral scissors.

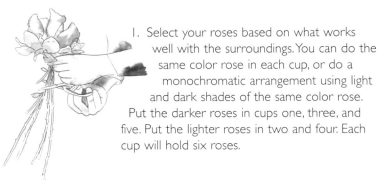

1. Select your roses based on what works
   well with the surroundings. You can do the
   same color rose in each cup, or do a
   monochromatic arrangement using light
   and dark shades of the same color rose.
   Put the darker roses in cups one, three, and
   five. Put the lighter roses in two and four. Each
   cup will hold six roses.

2. Cut the stems so that, when inserted
   into the cup, the mound of flower
   heads will show above the rim but
   the stems will be hidden.

3. Add pittosporum, hypericum, or
   Queen Anne's lace to the
   perimeter of the roses. Bind the
   bundle with a pipe cleaner.

4. Measure the bouquet again against the height of the cup to make sure the heads will now rest on the rim. Don't be shy about adjusting the positions of the flower heads so you have a nice tight mound of roses. If you ned to cut more length off the stems, do so, then drop the flowers into the cup. You can leave the pipe cleaner on because it won't show inside the cup.

5. Now array the five cups down the center of your dining table. You have a beautiful, simple, and original arrangement that people can admire during dinner but still easily see over.

Make it extra special ─────────────

If you like, you can also use a silver cordial at each place with one stem of Queen Anne's Lace and one rose in the center. For a more elaborate setting, add tall silver candlesticks or candelabrum to each end of the row of cups on your table.

Gladiola Basket

This is a nice arrangement for a round table.

You'll need: 8–12 gladiolas, a 6–8" container, knife, floral scissors, floral foam, a plastic liner, pipe cleaner, and raffia or wired ribbon.

1. In this arrangement we are using a wicker basket. Choose a liner to fit the basket. Cut floral foam to fit, place the foam in the liner, and secure. Place the liner with foam in the basket. Saturate the foam with water.

2. Take four full stems of gladiolas. Place two on one side of the container and two on the opposite side. Push them as far down into the floral foam as possible. Then pull each side to the center and join them to make a handle.

3. Secure the handle with a pipe cleaner. (You will cut it off later.)

Other ideas

Your container can be anything round—a silver bowl, clay pot, basket with no handle, or pottery bowl. Experiment with other flowers or greenery, too: Try a handle made from forsythia with daffodils in the base, or bells of Ireland for the handle and green roses for the base.

4. Insert remaining stems, that have been cut short, to cover the floral foam. If there is any remaining floral foam showing, add some greenery to the perimeter of the arrangement.

5. To finish, tie a couple of pieces of raffia around the stems at the top of the basket handle, or use wired ribbon to tie a bow. Then cut away the pipe cleaner and let the raffia or bow hold the handle secure.

Biedermeier Arrangement

Great for a buffet table or sideboard—wherever you need height.

You'll need: knife for cutting foam, hydrangea leaves or variegated hosta leaves, roses, single-bloom lilies, snapdragons, urn or other tall container with liner, floral foam, green floral tape.

1. Choose a liner to fit in your container—ours is an 8-inch liner. Cut heavy-duty floral foam to fit, place the foam in the liner, and secure with green waterproof floral tape. The tape helps stabilize the foam, which is important because of the weight of the flowers. Place the liner with foam in the container. Saturate the foam.

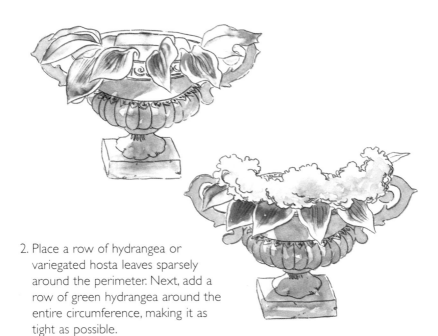

2. Place a row of hydrangea or variegated hosta leaves sparsely around the perimeter. Next, add a row of green hydrangea around the entire circumference, making it as tight as possible.

3. Add a row or two of roses just above the hydrangea heads—keep them tight.

4. Now add a row of single-bloom lilies.

5. Finally, add tall snapdragons, with all blooms exposed.

Simply beautiful secrets

About Biedermeier style

Originating in Switzerland in the late 1800s, this tightly-structured bouquet often had lemon and orange peels added for fragrance. The Biedermeier is showing signs of popularity again due to its dramatic geometry and pleasing symmetry.

This arrangement should be placed in an urn or something to add height. The finished arrangement should be about twenty-four to twenty-six inches above the container.

Roses in cups, with mini arrangements in cordials.

Gladiola basket (using ceramic container).

Biedermeier arrangement.

Bulb Arrangements

Bulbs (flowers grown from bulbs) are a flower-lover's best friend. They are relatively inexpensive, readily available much of the year, and easy to arrange. And there's nothing like a bouquet of bulbs for making a statement and brightening any room. Below are some helpful hints on dealing with bulbs, then specifics on arranging tulips, hyacinths, and irises. Think simple and sophisticated.

Tulips, daffodils, hyacinth, irises, and other typical spring bulbs need to be in water, since their stems are difficult to get into floral foam, and they just fare better in water. So choose containers that are deep enough to hold a lot of water. Measure the stems against the container to help you choose the right size.

Bulbs often have their own greenery, so it is not always necessary to add additional greenery to bulb arrangements.

Tulips

The secret to success here is to have enough tulips to fill the mouth of the vase so there is no movement.

You'll need: tulips (15–30), vase, and a knife.

1. Cut the tulips at a sharp angle and begin placing them around the perimeter of the vase.

2. Make another circle inside the first tulips. As you continue to place the tulips, they will form a kind of crisscrossing supporting grid with their stems.

3. You may have to wire the tulips that will go in the center, so their heads will stay up. Do this by inserting the top of the wire into the head where it meets the stem.

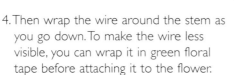

4. Then wrap the wire around the stem as you go down. To make the wire less visible, you can wrap it in green floral tape before attaching it to the flower.

5. Place the last few tulips in the vase. Insert them into the center of the arrangement. Because of the grid formed earlier, they will stay in place and fill the center.

Simply beautiful secrets ───────

Keep your tulips happy

Tulips tend to open in a warm environment. That does not mean they are old, just warm. By putting them in a cool place, even the refrigerator, they will close back into their original form.

Hyacinth

Hyacinth are wonderfully fragrant and mound nicely. Their stems are generally not more than ten to twelve inches, so you will need a shorter vase for this arrangement.

You'll need: hyacinth (10–15), vase, knife.

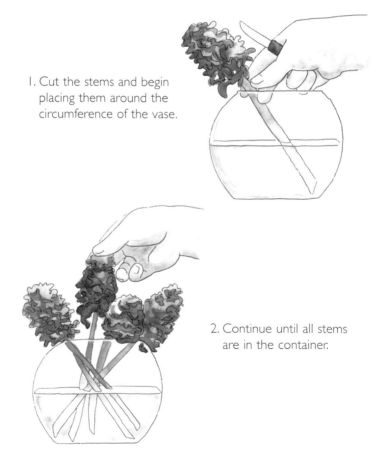

1. Cut the stems and begin placing them around the circumference of the vase.

2. Continue until all stems are in the container.

3. The last few stems in the center should be slightly higher to give a mounded effect rather than a flat effect.

Simply beautiful secrets

Bulb ordering tips

If you are planning for a special occasion or ordering flowers as a gift, and want a bulb flower like a tulip or hyacinth, remember the importance of seasonality. While you may be able to find flowers grown from bulbs during the off-season hot months, they will be in poor condition. Check the seasonal availability chart on pages 76–77 of this book and if your bulb flower is not in season, choose another flower that is.

Irises

Irises are wonderful flowers, but they do not have a long life so I tend to use them sparingly. Here is one of my favorite iris arrangements.

You'll need: irises (5), a pinholder frog, green floral tape, floral scissors, knife, a low wide container, some polished rocks or marbles, and some galax leaves, bear grass, or similar long slender greenery.

1. Fill your container with rocks.

2. Put irises on a pinholder frog, grouped together with the center iris slightly taller.

3. Place the frog with irises in the center of the container. If you can draw an imaginary triangle among any three of the flowers, your design is correct. If you can't do this, adjust as needed.

4. Place several stems of grass together for sturdiness and wrap them with stem tape (available from florists for this purpose).

Other ideas

If you choose not to use rocks, you can use a larger container, leave out the greenery, and fill the container with blueberries or lemons, with a few slices filling gaps between whole lemons. If you happen to own a decorative frog, you may not want to cover it up with either rocks or fruit, but let it show as part of the arrangement. To do this you would naturally have to be using a glass container like the one we are using here, or any container that happens to be see-through. You could even make an arrangement using multiple frogs and flowers, if the frogs are interesting and attractive.

5. Place the greenery in the frog. Add water to cover the stems.

Simply beautiful secrets

A note about arrangement proportions

As a general rule of thumb in planning your arrangements, the height of the arrangement should be one and one-half times the height of the container. But there are exceptions, such as the iris arrangement above. Notice that the height of the irises are more like three or four times as tall as the cylindrical glass bowl we have used as our container. In this instance, the proportionality is still acceptable because, although the container is low, it is unusually wide. Its width offsets the height of the flowers and bear grass used in the arrangement.

Tulip arrangement.

Hyacinth arrangement.

Irises with bear grass. Note rocks help disguise the frog.

Topiaries

Simple but sophisticated, a topiary is great in a foyer, in duplicate on a mantel, on a buffet table, even at a seated dinner because you can see around it.

You'll need: long-stemmed flowers (10 – 24), a 6" container, styrofoam, a plastic liner, floral foam, pipe cleaners, raffia, equestrian reeds (10 – 16), scissors, a knife, sheet moss, and floral wire.

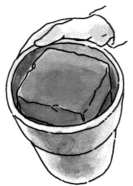

1. Place a chunk of styrofoam in the bottom of your container. (Terra cotta pots are wonderful for topiaries.) On top of the styrofoam, place a plastic liner. The size of the liner should match the bottom dimension of the container. If the bottom diameter is 6", you need a 6" diameter liner. In the liner, securely place floral foam, and water thoroughly.

2. Strip the leaves from your flowers. (You can leave a few around the flower heads for effect if you like.) Gather the flowers together tightly just beneath the flower heads and tie the stems together with a pipe cleaner.

3. Hold your tied bouquet against the container and cut the stems off even with the bottom of the floral foam. Then holding the flowers in both hands, push them firmly into the floral foam. Tighten and adjust the tie at the top if necessary to keep the topiary's shape.

4. Insert equestrian reeds, one at a time, into the floral foam flush against the "trunk" of the topiary. The reeds will be too long and will stick out at the top of the topiary so after inserting each one, cut it off at the top so the top end is hidden in the flowers. Encircle the trunk of the topiary in this way until it is encased in reeds.

Simply beautiful secrets

Floral foam: get it right the first time!
Remember that you only have one shot at securing your topiary flowers in the floral foam. So position carefully, then push the flowers in firmly. This is very important because if you do not do it correctly, you will have to get new floral foam and start over. The hole made by the bundle of flowers is so large that you can't reposition the flowers if it's not right.

5. To finish your topiary, tie raffia around the reeds at the top, just under the flower heads. (You may also want to tie it in a second or third location going down the stems, if you like the look of it or need it to help hold the reeds in place.) Then cut away the pipe cleaner. Put sheet moss around the base, covering the mouth of the container. Trim the moss off even with the lip of the container. To secure the moss, cut floral wire into pieces about 2" long and bend them into U-shapes like hairpins. Push them into the sheet moss and down into the floral foam. You can also use a dot of glue from your glue gun here and there to help adhere the moss to the lip of the container.

Other ideas

Sunflowers are my favorite topiary flower, but these arrangements are also lovely with dahlias, roses, daisies, lilies, alstroemeria, and even carnations. They give such a fresh contemporary look to any occasion. The topiary above is quite basic. If you like, you can make yours a little fancier by tying more raffia around the stems, adding a little more greenery to the flower mound at the top, or embellishing the base with additional blooms or greenery. There are really no limits to what you can do with a topiary, they are so versatile. So have fun!

— Rose Topiary —

First, decide how many roses to use. For six roses, use a four-inch clay rose pot; for twelve to eighteen roses, use a six-inch clay rose pot. Remove all the foliage from the rose stems and gather them into a ball. Tie them off with a pipe cleaner. Place the bundle of roses into the middle of the floral foam and push down firmly. Run larkspur, solidago, or hypericum up the stem just under the roses to form a cuff just beneath the flower heads. Finish covering the floral foam and add bows or raffia.

— Lily Topiary —

It is best to use 7–9 single-bloom lilies that are fresh, but fully open. If single blooms are not available, prune buds off the main stalk, leaving the lateral stems as long as possible. Then these buds can be used to decorate the base of the topiary. (Put them in before you add moss.) Remove all foliage. Make a circle in your hand, bringing each row of lilies down slightly to form a more balled effect. Proceed with topiary steps.

Sunflower topiary with equestrian reeds surrounding flower stems.

Rose topiary. Notice the flower stems remain exposed.

This lily topiary's base is embellished with added flowers and greenery.

Alstroemeria topiary. The urn gives it a more formal look.

Simply Festive Holiday Arrangements

Holidays mean a house full of good friends and family, so there is no better time to put your best flower arranging skills to work. It's also a time when most people are very busy, so remember to keep the flowers simple, elegant, fun, and unexpected. Here are five ideas to inspire you.

Easter

This versatile arrangement works for a seated dinner, buffet table, sideboard, foyer, or coffee table.

You'll need: a large tray, platter, or flat basket; three heads of Boston lettuce; two or three bunches of asparagus; three small bunches of spring flowers; three low containers (I often use votive candle holders); scissors and a knife; raffia; and your favorite Easter or spring collectible(s).

This is lovely, and it's easy to substitute for any of the elements you don't have. I like to use a wooden tray. Put three heads of Boston lettuce on the tray in a triangular form. Then disperse between the lettuce an arrangement of pink roses, an arrangement of hyacinth, and an arrangement of pink lilies. Place a bunny or other spring collectible on the tray wherever it looks nice. (You can put the lettuce in the refrigerator overnight if you want the arrangement to last for several days.) Finally, I like to add a couple of bunches of asparagus tied with raffia.

For another version of this, try starting with a pretty basket. Line it with a plastic liner, then add floral foam. Next, select a lovely dogwood branch or other spring flowering branch and shape it to fit the space. (The branch will have to be "conditioned." To do that, give it a clean angular cut, remove all foliage below the water line and let the branch sit in water for at least four hours.)

Place the branch firmly into the floral foam. Place a bunny at the base of the branch and add three to five tulips close together under the branch. Next, add three irises close together in another area. Finally, add a cluster of five hyacinth. Add a few stems of bear grass to each clump of flowers. Fill in with sheet moss and add brightly colored and decorated eggs in the spaces between the clumps of flowers.

Simply beautiful secrets ⎯⎯⎯⎯⎯⎯⎯⎯⎯⎯

Discover the treasures that are lying around your house
Take a fresh look around your house with your flower-arranging hat on, and you will find all sorts of things you can combine with flowers to get creative, personal effects. This Easter arrangement is a great example. If you have a collection of porcelain eggs, or ceramic flowers, or silver sugar bowls or creamers...whatever you collect and love, you can incorporate it into a simple arrangement like this to make it really yours. Add baby items for a shower, or bridal ones for a spring bridal tea. Whatever you use, you'll have a great centerpiece appropriate not only for Easter but any spring occasion.

Halloween

Try this miniature pumpkin and flower tree to liven up your autumnal table.

You'll need: 2–3 blocks of floral foam, floral scissors, a knife, chicken wire, a tray or platter to go under the tree, about 30 miniature pumpkins (depending on the size of your tree), unwired floral picks for each pumpkin, a piece of narrow dowel as long as your tree is tall, acrylic paints, greenery, and 15–25 roses, chrysanthemums, or other flowers of your choice.

1. Shape floral foam into a cone. Cut one block into a flat-topped cone shape, then cut two smaller blocks and set them on the top of the "tree."

2. Insert a thin dowel (smaller than a pencil in diameter) or bamboo reed down through the center of the foam pieces to hold them together. Floral supply dealers sell a slim green dowel called a hyacinth stake that is perfect for this purpose.

3. When the three pieces of foam are secured by the dowel, use your knife to finish trimming the top two pieces into a cone shape to form the top of your tree.

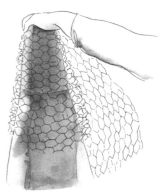

4. Wrap your cone "tree" securely in chicken wire.

5. Paint faces or other designs on each pumpkin (if desired). One at a time, insert a six-inch, unwired floral pick into the back side of each pumpkin and stick it into the floral foam. Put the sticks in at a slight angle so the chicken wire will help to support the weight of the pumpkin.

6. Place your tree on a round plate or platter, or other container that is slightly larger than the base of the tree. Make sure that whatever you use will hold water.

7. Finish your tree by filling in with flowers and greenery, using complementary fall tones. Fill in the edges of your container with flowers or greenery too.

8. When your tree is completed, water it thoroughly. Make sure all the foam is well saturated and that there is a little water in the container.

Simply beautiful secrets

For a dressier look

When I make this centerpiece I like to put black candles in clay pots on either side of it. You can even add black shades to the candles, if they are available. For a slightly more formal look, you can elevate the tree on a pedestal or put it in an urn.

Thanksgiving

My favorite Thanksgiving arrangement involves a combination of vegetables and flowers. It's simple and great for any fall occasion.

You'll need: a large tray or platter, floral scissors, a knife, two or three small bunches of fall flowers, two or three different vegetables to make into "vases," three artichokes, other assorted fall vegetables depending on your taste, and 3 votive candles or tea lights.

First, choose a number of vegetables that would be suitable to hold flowers, and some that can be used to flank those. Then choose your tray; I suggest copper or wood rather than silver. Good choices of vegetables to hold flowers are eggplant, cabbage or lettuce, acorn squash, and artichokes. To flank the flowers, you can use turnips, squash, parsnips, and red leaf lettuce.

Level the vegetables that are going to be used for containers. To do this, first cut a piece off the bottom so the vegetable "vase" will sit upright. Then cut off the tops, and with your knife carefully scoop out enough of the vegetable to insert a piece of heavy floral foam. Be sure to leave a thick wall of the vegetable so that it will be able to support the floral foam and the flowers. Add water to saturate the floral foam.

Next, add the flowers. I like to use sunflowers in the squash (with the heads sitting just above the opening), orange roses in the lettuce, and hypericum in the eggplant. Group the flowers in a triangle, leaving some of the tray exposed. Then tuck turnips and parsnips or squash around the flowers. If you want to use candles, level three to five artichokes and remove the center. Then place a plastic encased disposable votive in each one, and add them to the tray of vegetables and flowers. On the next page, I'll show you in more detail how to make the artichoke "candle holders." (These are something you can make and use almost any time of year!)

1. Start with a large, fresh, firm artichoke.

2. Cut off the stem and any bottom leaves that need to come off to make the artichoke sit upright on a tabletop.

3. With your knife, hollow out the center of the artichoke. Hollow out just the amount of space you will need to hold your votive candle securely.

4. Set the votive candle in the artichoke. When you have finished making all your artichoke candleholders, set them in among the other flowers and vegetables in your Thanksgiving arrangement.

Christmas

Because there are so many other decorations in the house at Christmas, I keep the flowers simple. This arrangement only looks like you spent a lot of time arranging!

You'll need: a ring of floral foam; 1–2 dozen roses and spray roses, depending on ring size; a round tray to place under the ring; holly; sheet moss; floral scissors; knife; floral wire; a large pillar candle and hurricane globe, if desired.

1. Cut the stems short on your roses and insert them into the top and outer wall of the saturated floral foam ring. I like to mix spray roses with the standard red roses to add texture. Spray roses have multiple blooms on one stem. You can use a lot of roses and a little greenery in this arrangement, or fewer roses and more greenery, it all depends on your personal taste.

2. When you've got all the roses placed where you want them, fill in with greenery. I like to use variegated holly but you can use whatever you like.

3. If there are empty spaces anywhere, continue to fill in with flowers or greenery. You want to cover all the floral foam. For the inside of the ring, I like to make it easier by covering it with sheet moss. Just bend about a 2" piece of floral wire into a hairpin shape, take a piece of moss, and secure it to the inner wall of the ring with your wire hairpin. Continue until you've covered the entire inner wall of the ring with sheet moss.

4. I always set the finished wreath on a round tray or platter to protect my tabletop. The rings come with an attached plastic base but it isn't enough to protect a table. After setting the wreath on its tray, take a hurricane globe with a tall pillar candle (in whatever colors work with your decor) and place it in the center.

5. If you don't have a hurricane globe, you can stand your favorite Christmas figure in the center of the wreath or use just a plain pillar candle.

Simply beautiful secrets

Keep your wreath happy

Because the floral foam ring does not have an ongoing water source, it is necessary to resaturate it every day. Just place the entire ring in a shallow amount of water — enough to cover the ring, not the flowers — and let it sit for 15 minutes. Because the flowers are cut so short, they will last more than a week.

Hanukkah

**This easy arrangement incorporates the traditional colors of
Hanukkah, white and blue.
For a beautiful presentation, situate the menorah on a
sideboard with a low arrangement of white roses mounded in
the container, then add dark blue delphiniums all around
the perimeter of the roses.**

You'll need: a menorah and candles, 12–15 white roses, 8–12 blue
delphiniums, a short container, a pipe cleaner, aspidistra leaves or other
broad leaves to line the container if it is glass (hiding the tied-together
rose stems).

The secret to this is to cut the rose stems short and tie them tightly
with a pipe cleaner as you did with the Roses in Cups arrangement.
Drop the roses into your container and place the delphiniums around
the edges of the rose bundle.

Simply beautiful secrets

Hints and tips on long-distance flower ordering

Ordering flowers bound for another city can be tricky, particularly if you don't know your flowers. If you call a local florist to place the order for you, be very specific. Tell them what you want or don't want – no carnations or mums, for instance. Try to stick to simpler arrangements, such as a dozen red tulips. There is no chance for error that way, and you have recourse if they are not sent.

You can also order flowers online, but again, you'll need to be careful because quality control is often a problem. If you want to send something special, we recommend using the wire service "b. brooks Fine Flowers." They are an online service for both fine florists and discerning customers. You can call them at 888-346-3356, or go online at www.bbrooks.com. Their web site is a little different from most in that it is service-oriented. The photos on the site are more illustrative of the type of arrangements that fine florists do, and are meant to serve as a guide to style and pricing. The easiest way to use the site is simply to go to "orders" and write in what you want, the occasion, and adjust the price to what you want to spend. Be sure to give a phone number(s) where you can be reached in case there are questions about your order.

Remember, most florists have a cut-off for same-day delivery – typically it is noon in the recipient's zone. If you want something very specific, give the florist a couple of days to get what you want. Otherwise, provide alternate choices. Most fine florists have a $50 minimum, plus tax and delivery.

For worldwide delivery, I suggest contacting a florist who is a member of Teleflora (just ask when you call). This is one of the largest wire services and membership assures you of a basic level of professionalism and accountability that you might not find elsewhere.

Dorothy's Q & A

Here are answers to some of the questions that I have been asked repeatedly over the years, along with many helpful hints that will have you on your way to successful flower arranging. I hope at least a few of your questions are answered here, too.

Is there a rule about the height of the flower arrangement in proportion to the container?

When in doubt, $1^1/_2$ times the height of the container is safe and proportionate. You can certainly go taller; and sometimes, I sit a blossom directly on top of the vase. The biggest no-no is: Never make the arrangement the height of the container, because it will look boxy.

Do you need to cut flowers underwater?
It is not imperative, but it helps to avoid air blocks in the stem, thus improving the life of the flower. Most professionals do process flowers underwater.

What type of floral foam should I use for heavy stems?
There are two types of foam: One is lightweight (instant) and has holes across the surface for fast saturation; the other is heavy duty (deluxe) and has no holes, so it takes longer to saturate. For heavy stems, use the heavier version and cover it with chicken wire to help support the stems. Place the foam in clean water to which you have added flower food. Never press it down; just let it float. It will sink when it is fully saturated.

What is sheet moss, where do I find it, and how should I store it?
This is the moss you see in the woods growing in sheets on the ground. Florists and hobby and craft stores sell it. Store it in a plastic zip-top bag in the fridge. You can spritz it with water mixed with a few drops of green food coloring if it turns brown.

What can I do to get my glass containers clean?
First, change the water in your arrangements regularly and wash the containers immediately after use. If, however, you develop scum in the container, get Efferdent® (this is a product used to clean false teeth, but its effervesce cleans almost anything). Put a tablet in the container and add hot water. Let it sit in the container for about 30 minutes. Repeat, if necessary.

I have many glass and crystal containers that I like to use, but sometimes I want to make arrangements that need floral foam. How can I cover floral foam?

Insert tall green leaves around the floral foam, allowing the tips to extend beyond the mouth of the container. Cut the bottom of the leaves straight, using the container to measure. For a bowl, wrap leaves horizontally around the foam.

Can you put flowers around or on food for decoration?

Yes, but only certain ones. They include banana leaves, pansies, nasturtiums, chrysanthemums, hibiscus, lavender, lilies, roses, and all herbs, many of which have blooms. Be sure to spray the flowers with fresh water to dislodge any residue if they are to be eaten. Some of these flowers are organically grown and sold specifically for garnish. Be sure to check with a poison control center if you have any question about a flower because there are some beautiful blooms that are poisonous.

How do you remove lily stain?

Always remove the stamens because the pollen will stain. Also, removing the pollen extends the life of the lily. I usually wear plastic gloves, and gently pull the stamens out. If you do get a stain, do not rub it in. Get a pipe cleaner and brush the pollen or get a piece of tape and gently pull the pollen off. Remove as much pollen as possible and wash according to fabric directions.

Is adding Sprite® or aspirin good for extending the life of roses?

Possibly, I don't know. What I do know is that commercial flower food (or preservative) is perfectly formulated to extend flower life – no guessing. Cutting the stems every couple of days at an angle, adding preservative, cleaning the container, and adding fresh water works every time. In lieu of the preservative (which, by the way, is available in any florist shop) two or three drops of Clorox in a quart of water will help to reduce the bacteria in the water.

Can clay pots be used in dressier settings?
I love using clay pots for arrangements and plants. They come in so many sizes and shapes, from one inch to sixty inches in diameter. They appear in all kinds of settings and seem to adapt to the mood of the room. I prefer the ones that are aged.

The aged pots I've seen are costly. Is there a way I can age pots myself?
Put them in a damp, shady area in your yard and, over time, they will be aged and mossy looking. For quicker results, get a wide paintbrush and cover the pots with buttermilk and, again, leave them in a shady damp place. Repeat this procedure two or three times and in about two weeks, they should be mossy. Then dry them out in the sun before using. Probably a few hours on a sunny day will be sufficient.

Do blooming branches last well in arrangements?
Many do, and increasingly more are available on the commercial market. For example, you should be able to find forsythia, dogwood, quince, cherry, and crape myrtle. I like these best dropped in a vase with no other greenery. It may be necessary to prune the lateral branches on some stems to give you a cleaner, more vertical look. Cut the branches with sharp shears and remove any lower foliage. Then put them in deep water for at least four hours before transferring to a vase or floral foam.

What are some of your favorite flowers that are less common?
Lisianthus — It is graceful and lovely. It is affectionately known as "little lizzies." I remember years ago speaking to Medical Wives of Mississippi, and the actress Patricia Neal was the inspirational

speaker. She spoke first and then, much to my surprise, came to see my demonstration. She was smitten with the lisianthus, and we eventually sent her seed. Ultimately, she opened an account with us and had us send vases and other flower tools to her, and often, to her friends. It has the same effect on lots of people, and it is simple to arrange.

Peonies — I love them because they are so opulent looking.

Queen Anne's Lace — I like it just dropped into an earthenware pitcher or a tall silver vase

Is it true that flowers you purchase should be kept in a cooler?
Housing flowers in a cooler really is important to their life cycle. Flowers lose water vapor in elevated temperatures. Like a person's skin, moisture is lost through all of the flower surfaces when exposed to high temperatures. For example, flowers held at 50 degrees deteriorate three times faster than those held at 32 to 34 degrees. In most outdoor markets and grocery stores, the temperature could be 70 to 90 degrees. The result is greatly reduced shelf life for the flowers.

What is ethylene gas? I have heard that it is bad for flowers.
Ethylene gas is a colorless, odorless gas that fresh produce emits as it ripens. The small amount that is released by ripening fruit is not harmful to people or pets. It is, however, extremely harmful to cut flowers, and shortens the life. The next time you are in a grocery store, check the proximity of the flowers to the produce.

How can I sharpen my floral tools?
You can purchase a small tool sharpener at some hardware stores, and there are places like old-time hobby stores and bicycle shops that still sharpen tools. Often, however, the cost doesn't warrant sharpening, and tools such as clippers are best replaced. It really is

important to have sharp tools because cutting with a dull or poorly designed tool could crush the stem rather than making a clean cut, thereby injuring the flower and decreasing its vigor.

How much greenery should I remove from a flower stem?
Remove any foliage that would be below the water level. Beyond that, remove any leaf that would obscure another flower or does not look appropriate in the arrangement. I find that most beginning arrangers tend to use more greenery than is necessary.

How can I determine how much to cut off my flower stems before arranging them?
The simplest way is to hold the stems on the outside of the container at the height that looks desirable and make the cut. When in doubt, leave the stem a little longer. You can always recut it. Remember it is best to design the flowers in the space they will occupy so you can see the arrangement in relation to the space available.

If I buy flowers loose, is it okay to transport them out of water?
If you are only going a short distance, it is okay. But remember to recut the stems at an angle, underwater if possible, and add flower food. Never leave fresh flowers in a parked car for long periods of time because the heat and lack of air circulation is very damaging.

How can I transport flowers that are in a vase?
A good way is to get a box that has dividers, and put vases or clay pots in those to transport. We also use cinder blocks, because they are so heavy. We wrap the opening in paper or bubble wrap and put the vase in the center; it makes for a very secure ride.

Flower Availability

	NAME	DESCRIPTION	COLORS	
1.	Alstroemeria	clusters of trumpet-shaped flowers bi-colors	orange, pink, red, purple, white and	
2.	Bells of Ireland	tall line flowers that are cup-shaped	lime green	
3.	Calla Lily	curvy flower, smooth stem	white, green, yellow, magenta, orange	
4.	Delphinium	clusters of small blooms very dense on a tall stem	white, light blue, dark blue and pink	
5.	Gerbera daisy	large daisy-like bloom with layers of petals	white, yellow, red, magenta, orange, coral, apricot, green and many bicolors	
6.	Gladiolus	Medium-sized blooms on a tall stem	white, green, yellow, orange, coral, magenta, pink, red, lavender, purple and many bi-colors	
7.	Hyacinth	Small, firm blooms on a short stem	white, blue, pink, yellow, purple and lavender	
8.	Hydrangea	Large, round flowers; dense clusters of small petals	blue, white, green, lavender and pink	
9.	Hypericum	cluster of berries	reddish brown, apricot and green	
10.	Iris	single large bloom	white, yellow, blue, purple and lavender	
11.	Larkspur	small clusters of flowers on a tall stem	purple, lavender, pink, white,	
12.	Lily – Asiatic	large, showy single to five blooms per stem; trumpet-shaped flowers; Asiatic lilies are not fragrant	white, cream, yellow, pink, red, orange	
13.	Lily – Oriental	very large, showy blooms one to five blooms per stem; trumpet-shaped flowers; Oriental lilies are very fragrant	white, pink, cream, and many bicolors; the best known of these lilies is the stargazer, which is white with an intense rich rose center	
14.	Lisianthus	Multi-cupped blooms on a stem	white, pink, lavender, purple, green and bi-colors	
15.	Peony	very large flower; single or double (higher petal count)	white, pink, magenta, and red	
16.	Queen Anne's Lace	tiny, delicate flowers that form a large head	white	
17.	Rose	single flower; dense petal count	white, pink, yellow, orange, red, terra cotta, apricot, coral, lavender, violet and many, many bicolors	
18.	Snapdragon	multiple small blooms on tall stem	white, pink, yellow, orange, red, magenta and some bicolors	
19.	Stock	clusters of small blooms on a stem	white, cream, lavender, purple, pink, magenta	
20.	Sunflower	large flower; bright petals surrounding dark centers	yellow, red, bronze-brown	
21.	Tulip	single bloom	white, yellow, pink, coral, orange, red, lavender, purple and many bicolors	
22.	Waxflower	tiny clusters of waxy flowers	white, purple and pink	
23.	Zinnia	single bloom	white, cream, pink, purple, peach, orange, yellow and red	

See key on next page for flower identification

LIFE	MEANING	AVAILABILITY	TYPE
6–14 days	Devotion	Year-round	Perennial
7–10 days	Good luck	Year-round	Annual
7–10 days	Beauty	Year-round	Perennial Rhizome
5–10 days	Fickleness, levity	Year-round	Perennial
5–8 days	Friendship	Year-round	Perennial
7–10 days	Sincerity	Year-round	Bulb
5–8 days	Kindliness	October-June	Bulb
4–8 days	Understanding	Year-round	Shrub
7–14 days		Year-round	Perennial
3–6 days	Promise	Year-round	Bulb or Rhizome
6–14 days	Fickleness, levity	Year-round	Annual
7–14 days	Purity: white; Gratitude: yellow; Burning Desire: orange	Year-round	Bulb
7–14 days	Same as Asiatic	Year-round	Bulb
7–14 days	Showy	Year-round	Annual
5–10 days	Compassion	May-June	Perennial Shrub
5–10 days	Haven	Year-round	Biennial
3–14 days	Love: red; Friendship: pink; Purity: white: purity; Jealousy: Yellow	Year-round	Shrub
5–10 days	Strength	Year-round	Annual
5–8 days	Lasting beauty	Year-round	Annual
5–10 days	Pride	May-November for large variety, smaller flowers are available year-round	Some varieties are perennials, some annuals; check before purchasing.
5–7 days	Perfect lover	October-May	Bulb
7–12 days	Unknown	Year-round	Shrub
4–7 days	Daily remembrance	June-September	Annual

Flower Identification

1. Alstroemeria

2. Bells of Ireland

3. Calla Lily

4. Delphinium

5. Gerbera daisy

6. Gladiolus

7. Hyacinth

8. Hydrangea

9. Hypericum

10. Iris

11. Larkspur

12. Lily – Asiatic

13. Lily – Oriental

14. Lisianthus

15. Peony

16. Queen Anne's Lace

17. Rose

18. Snapdragon

19. Stock

20. Sunflower

21. Tulip

22. Waxflower

23. Zinnia

Bibliography

Botanica's Annuals and Perennials. San Diego, Calif.: Laurel Glen Publishing, 1999.

Cathey, Dr. H. Marc. *Heat-Zone Gardening,* China: Time-Life Books, 1998.

Leggatt, Jenny. *Cooking with Flowers.* New York: Ballantine Books, 1987.

Packer, Jane. *The Complete Guide to Flower Arranging.* New York: Dorling Kindersley Publishing, 1995.

Packer, Jane. *Jane Packer's New Flower Arranging.* North Pomfret, Vt.: Trafalgar Square Publishing, 1994.

Pryke, Paula. *Flowers, Flowers!* New York: Rizzoli International Publications, Inc., 1993.

About the Author

DOROTHY SARRIS McDANIEL is the owner of Dorothy McDaniel's Flower Market in Birmingham, Alabama. Although she holds a degree in criminology, she has made her career in professional floral design for more than 25 years. A veteran public speaker and broadcast spokesperson on the subject of flowers and flower arranging, she has over the years appeared as a regular guest demonstrator for the Macy's and Rich's department store chain and been interviewed by many newspapers and television and radio programs. Her popular floral designs and advice on flower arranging have appeared on the pages of *Southern Living, Southern Accents, Cooking Light, Creative Ideas for Living,* and *Portico* magazines. Although flowers are her life's work, Dorothy McDaniel still finds time to pursue her other passions: fly fishing, upland bird hunting, opera, reading, and cooking. This is her first book.